Buffalo
Soldiers

Catherine Reef

Twenty-First Century Books

A Division of Henry Holt and Company
New York

PHOTO CREDITS

cover: flag by Fred J. Eckert/FPG International; photo courtesy US Army Military History Institute. **3:** Larry Schwarm/Courtesy of the Buffalo Soldier Monument Committee. **4, 6:** National Archives. **12:** National Archives. **14, 17:** Shomburg Center for Research in Black Culture. **18:** National Archives. **23:** Schomburg Center for Research in Black Culture. **25:** Bettmann. **27:** Schomburg Center for Research in Black Culture. **30:** National Archives. **32:** Schomburg Center for Research in Black Culture. **35:** Bettmann. **36:** Library of Congress. **37:** Bettmann. **42:** National Archives. **45:** Bettmann. **48, 49:** National Archives. **51:** Bettmann. **57:** National Archives. **60, 62:** National Archives. **65, 68:** UPI/Bettmann. **69:** Bettmann. **75:** Larry Schwarm/Courtesy of the Buffalo Soldier Monument Committee.

Twenty-First Century Books
A Division of Henry Holt and Company, Inc.
115 West 18th Street
New York, NY 10011

Henry Holt® and colophon are registered trademarks of
Henry Holt and Company, Inc.
Publishers since 1866.

Published in Canada by Fitzhenry & Whiteside Ltd.,
91 Granton Drive, Richmond Hill, Ontario L4B 2N5

Library of Congress Cataloging-in-Publication Data

Reef, Catherine
Buffalo soldiers / Catherine Reef. — 1st ed.
p.   cm. — (African-American soldiers)
Includes biographical references and index.
Summary: Recounts the deeds of the 9th and 10th Cavalry, comprised of
African-American soldiers who kept peace between Indians and settlers on
the western frontier, fought in the Spanish-American War, and pursued the
outlaw Pancho Villa through Mexico.
1. Afro-Americans—West (U.S.)—History—19th century—Juvenile
literature. 2. Afro-American soldiers—West (U.S.)—History—19th
century—Juvenile literature. 3. United States. Army—Afro-American
troops—History—19th century—Juvenile literature. 4. Frontier and pioneer
life—West (U.S.)—Juvenile literature. 5. Indians of North
America—Wars—1866-1895—Juvenile literature. 6. West
(U.S.)—History—1848-1950—Juvenile literature. 7. United States. Army.
Cavalry, 9th—Juvenile literature. 8. United States. Army. Cavalry,
10th—Juvenile literature.
[1. Afro-Americans—History—19th century. 2. Afro-American
soldiers—History—19th century. 3. United States. Army. Cavalry, 9th.
4. United States. Army. Cavalry, 10th.]
I. Title. II. Series.
E185.925.R44 1993
978'.00496073—dc20   92-34413 CIP AC

ISBN 0-8050-2372-0
First Edition—1993

Printed in Mexico
All first editions are printed on acid-free paper ∞.
10 9 8 7 6 5 4 3 2 1

Contents

Chapter 1

The Story Behind the Paintings

"To be with you all is something very special for me." It was July 28, 1990. General Colin Powell spoke to a crowd of two thousand people gathered on a hillside at Fort Leavenworth, Kansas.

This busy Army post covers seven thousand acres. Every day, soldiers march in formation along its miles of roads. Officers come to Fort Leavenworth to study military tactics at the Army Command and Staff College.

In the 1800s, Fort Leavenworth was nothing more than a group of whitewashed buildings sitting on the prairie. During that century when many Americans moved west, the fort served as the Army's main outpost along the lonely route to New Mexico and Arizona.

Administration Building, Fort Leavenworth, Kansas, 1884

General Colin Powell

Fort Leavenworth is remembered, too, as the birthplace of the Buffalo Soldiers. It was there, in 1866, that the historic 10th Cavalry was formed. This unit of soldiers on horseback was one of four regiments called Buffalo Soldiers—black men who served on the western frontier.

In July 1990, Colin Powell had come to Fort Leavenworth to honor these men.

Powell is one of the best-known soldiers in the nation. He was the first African American to hold his country's highest military position, chairman of the Joint Chiefs of Staff. On that hot summer day, he had joined his fellow Americans to break ground for a Buffalo Soldier Monument. Soon, on the spot where the crowd had gathered, a statue of a Buffalo Soldier would stand more than twelve feet tall.

The general surveyed the crowd as he stood at the podium. Among the honored guests who sat near General Powell were William Harrington and Elisha Kearse, men who had retired from service with the black cavalry regiments. "Both Buffalo Soldiers are ninety-five years young," Powell said. "We can only marvel at the things they've seen."

"The Buffalo Soldiers are but a symbol, just one chapter in a proud and glorious history," Powell told the crowd. "To remind me of that history, I have a Buffalo Soldier painting that hangs on a wall in my office directly across from my desk." The painting, said Powell, shows a band of Buffalo Soldiers riding together on a patrol.

Across the Great Plains—from the Dakotas to Texas, from Kansas to the Rocky Mountains—the Buffalo Soldiers defended people, settlements, and livestock. They patrolled the western deserts. They searched for outlaws who preyed upon stagecoaches and frontier dwellings. They made sure that western settlers obeyed the law.

Outlaws were not the only threat the Buffalo Soldiers faced. The harsh desert environment also presented dangers. Temperatures could rise above one hundred degrees Fahrenheit during the day, and plunge below freezing at night. Getting lost in the desert could mean dying of thirst.

"I have another Buffalo Soldier painting in my office," Powell continued. "It depicts a young Buffalo Soldier and a Seminole Indian scout on the western plains."

Although some Native Americans worked as scouts for the soldiers, most were on the opposing side in the conflicts known as the Indian Wars. The Buffalo Soldiers are best known for acting with courage in this fierce struggle that pitted the United States government against the Indian tribes native to America.

The settlers who were moving west had their

eye on land—land that had long been home to the native people. The American government uprooted many tribes from their homes. United States forces killed thousands of Native Americans. They herded the rest onto areas called reservations. When the Indians fought to preserve their way of life, the Americans called them savages.

The Buffalo Soldiers rode into this tragic episode in American history. It is an odd twist of fate, many people point out, that these men, members of a race that spent generations in slavery, helped to take freedom from another group of people.

The Buffalo Soldiers did not seek opportunities to kill or capture Indians, however. They tried most of all to keep peace between Indians and settlers. But when a fight could not be avoided, they defended the citizens of their country, the United States of America.

These black men in uniform were among the many thousands of people of every race who helped to build the United States. They were soldiers doing their duty, Americans serving their country. They served with pride and patriotism even when their country treated them unfairly.

For many years, the Army's leaders refused to promote black soldiers to positions of command and gave them second-rate supplies. Often, the white settlers—people the Buffalo Soldiers risked their lives to protect—expressed their hatred of African Americans.

When their busy years on the frontier ended, the Buffalo Soldiers continued to serve. In 1898, they fought in Cuba during the Spanish-American War. They helped to win the most famous battle of that war, the assault on San Juan Hill.

"I have a third painting," Colin Powell told his audience. "The third painting that hangs in my office shows San Juan Hill as it should be shown—with black and white soldiers together seizing that hill on a muggy, hot July day in 1898."

"These three paintings in my office make interesting subjects of conversation when important visitors come to see me," Powell said. "I tell them the story behind the paintings."

The story Powell tells begins with the founding of the United States of America. It is the story of black soldiers fighting to defend their country and gain opportunities in the armed forces. It is a story that includes the Buffalo Soldiers and the first black chairman of the Joint Chiefs of Staff.

"I know I wouldn't be able to tell that story, I wouldn't be where I am today," said Powell, "if thousands of African Americans had not prepared the way for me. And among the thousands, planted firmly like a great fort on the western desert, stand the Buffalo Soldiers—an everlasting symbol of man's ability to overcome, an everlasting symbol of human courage in the face of all obstacles and dangers."

Chapter 2

Soldiers of the U.S. Army

On a warm day in 1876, General William Hoffman, commander of Fort Leavenworth, prepared to review his troops.

Hundreds of soldiers stood at attention in long, straight rows. Their heavy blue uniforms grew more uncomfortable as the minutes passed. The regiments, or units of soldiers, at last received orders to march. One after another, they paraded past the general.

One regiment, however, stood apart from the rest. Fort Leavenworth's lone regiment of black soldiers stood at parade rest—feet apart, hands behind their backs. Hoffman had ordered the 10th Cavalry not to march.

Like the white soldiers, the men of the 10th Cavalry had volunteered to serve their country. But unlike the white soldiers, the black cavalrymen received treatment that made them feel unwelcome.

The Army outfitted its black soldiers with old rifles and worn-out horses. General Hoffman assigned the 10th Cavalry to quarters in a low, swampy area. Disease-causing bacteria thrived in the dampness, and some of the men caught pneumonia.

Colonel Benjamin Grierson, the 10th Cavalry's white leader, complained about the treatment his soldiers received. But the Army ignored

Colonel Benjamin
Grierson

his protests. He objected, too, to the Army's name for his regiment—the 10th Colored Cavalry. "You will not refer to this regiment as the 10th Colored Cavalry, but as the 10th Cavalry," he instructed the officers who served under him. "Regardless of their colored skins, they are soldiers of the U.S. Army."

Grierson had not planned to become a cavalry soldier. When he was eight years old, a horse kicked him in the face. The injury left him scarred and fearful of horses. He overcame his fear of horses when he joined the Army during the Civil War.

More than 200,000 African Americans fought for the United States in that war, which lasted from 1861 until 1865. Thirty-eight thousand lost their lives. After the Civil War ended, the government decided, for the first time, to allow black men to serve in the armed forces during peacetime. The Army needed soldiers as a peacekeeping force in the west. And African Americans had shown their courage and ability to follow orders.

The government formed four black regiments. They were the 9th and 10th Cavalry, and the 24th and 25th Infantry, which were two units of foot soldiers. White officers served with these regiments, because the Army would not permit blacks to command troops.

This drawing by famous artist Frederic Remington shows a soldier of the 10th Cavalry.

To the 12,500 newly enlisted black men, the Army offered steady pay, as well as food, clothing, and shelter. It offered an opportunity for a career. "I got tired of looking mules in the face from sunrise to sunset," said Charles Creek, a farm laborer who signed up. "There must be a better living in this world."

14

Farmers, servants, and wagon drivers volunteered, along with house painters, cooks, and cigar makers. Some of the new soldiers, such as William Christy of Pennsylvania, hoped to see more of the country than the farmland where they had grown up. Some were like Thomas Shaw, who had fought in the Civil War and wanted to continue his military service. Others were more like Emanuel Stance of South Carolina. Nineteen years old and barely five feet tall, Stance was looking for adventure.

Whatever their reasons for enlisting, these men joined a proud tradition of African-American service in the U.S. military. From the time of the American Revolution, black soldiers and sailors have been among the heroes of every American war.

On March 5, 1770, a tall, husky former slave named Crispus Attucks became the first person to die in the American struggle for independence. Attucks led an angry mob through the streets of Boston to protest the presence of armed British troops. The crowd taunted the red-coated soldiers. When the soldiers raised their guns and fired into the crowd, Attucks met his death.

Peter Salem was another hero of the American Revolution. At the Battle of Bunker Hill, Salem shot and killed a British major, John Pitcairn, and so helped to win that important battle.

Three decades after the Revolution ended, a black sailor named John Johnson distinguished himself. Johnson served aboard an American ship in the War of 1812. The United States fought this war with England for the right to sail the ocean undisturbed. Many key battles of the War of 1812 took place on the water.

While battling on Lake Erie, Johnson was struck by British gunfire. He lay dying on the ship's deck, yet he urged his fellow sailors to keep on fighting. The ship's commander, Nathan Shaler, said that Johnson should be "remembered with reverence as long as bravery is considered a virtue."

Black soldiers helped General Andrew Jackson win the Battle of New Orleans, a major battle of the War of 1812. Jackson's men faced an attacking British force led by General Edward Parkenham. One of Jackson's African-American soldiers, a man that Jackson called a "famous rifle shot," took aim and fired. His bullet hit its target, and Parkenham fell dead.

Twice, African Americans had helped their nation achieve victory—in the Revolution and the War of 1812. But as soon as the United States was at peace, the Army closed its doors to blacks. "No Negro," stated an Army policy adopted in 1820, "will be received as a recruit of the Army."

And by the time the Civil War began, black

men had been barred from the service for more than forty years. Many white Americans doubted their ability to fight.

At first, some people called this conflict between the North and the South "the white man's war." Whites in the North expected the war to end quickly, and thought that they could win it themselves. But when the Civil War turned out to be a long conflict with a high death toll, the white Northerners knew they needed help. The government asked African Americans to join the fight.

Nearly 200,000 men enlisted in all-black regiments of the Union, or U.S., Army, and served under white officers. A handful of African Americans achieved officers' ranks during the Civil War, but they did not command troops. The nation's leaders believed that blacks lacked the needed skills and experience.

African Americans took part in more than four hundred Civil War battles. One of those battles occurred at New Market Heights, Virginia, a small town nestled between the Blue Ridge and Appalachian mountains.

At dawn on September 29, 1864, nine black regiments were among the Northern forces that marched toward the town. The Southern, or Confederate, Army showered them with bullets, and

Major Martin Delany served as a medical officer in the Civil War.

17

many soldiers lost their lives. Instead of scaring off the Union men, though, the gunfire brought out their courage. By the next day, the Union had captured New Market Heights. The commanding General, Benjamin Butler, knew that he owed this victory to the courage of his black troops. No longer could anyone doubt their ability to fight, he believed. Butler said it this way: "I felt in my inmost heart that the capacity of the Negro race for soldiers had then and there been fully satisfied forever."

One of the best-known Civil War regiments was the 54th Massachusetts Colored Infantry, which led the assault on Fort Wagner in South Carolina. Attacking at twilight on July 18, 1863, the 54th's soldiers charged bravely in the face of enemy gunfire. "Not a man flinched," wrote a soldier named Lewis Douglass, "though it was a trying time."

The assault on Fort Wagner

Sergeant William Carney of the 54th Infantry became the first African American to earn the Congressional Medal of Honor, awarded for bravery in battle. On that historic night in South Carolina, he carried the Union flag to the front of the attack on Fort Wagner. All through the fight, even though bullets struck him, Carney held the flag high. Visible only in the light of exploding artillery fire, the stars and stripes gave courage to the Northern soldiers.

When the Civil War ended, African Americans prepared to serve their country on the western frontier. While the 10th Cavalry was forming in Kansas, the 9th Cavalry, another black regiment, took shape in Louisiana.

Colonel Edward Hatch commanded the 9th Cavalry. Born in Maine, the blond, blue-eyed Hatch had earned a medal for bravery in the Civil War. He was known as a strong leader and a man who could make quick decisions.

The new soldiers learned to follow orders and perform complicated drills. They practiced handling their horses and weapons. In the summer of 1867, they received orders to move out to frontier Army posts. The 9th and 10th Cavalry went west to join the conflicts known as the Indian Wars.

Chapter 3

The West

The black cavalrymen rode into a tense and violent situation. The 9th Cavalry staffed forts in Texas, where the Kiowa and Comanche tribes were fighting with settlers. Men of the 10th Cavalry went to forts throughout Kansas. There, the soldiers made sure that travelers in stagecoaches and covered wagons reached their destinations safely.

Some 10th Cavalry soldiers went to Indian Territory, to try to prevent fighting there. The government had set aside this land, in present-day Oklahoma, for the Indians' use.

From their lonely western outposts, the men of the 9th and 10th Cavalry looked out on miles of open land. They saw settlers arriving in mule-drawn wagons. To the settlers, the land seemed free for the taking.

The settlers cared little that the plots on which they built houses and planted farms were home to Native-American tribes. As they plowed up grassland and laid down railroad tracks, they disturbed the Indians' way of life. It was a way of life with close ties to the natural world. The tribes of the plains followed the great buffalo herds and took from nature only what they needed.

The settlers belonged to a culture that valued progress and profits. They were eager to take advantage of the west's abundant resources. Only the Indians prevented the people of the United States from seizing these riches.

In the early 1800s, President Andrew Jackson spoke for many Americans. The American people had a duty, Jackson said, to bring a "dense and civilized population" to a land where only "a few savage hunters" lived.

The "civilized population," however, exposed the native people to technology, manufactured goods, whiskey, and diseases. Life would never be the same for the Native Americans.

This clash of cultures was nothing new. Native Americans began losing their world to white settlers in the 1600s, when the first shiploads of Europeans arrived on the East Coast. The Pequamid people welcomed the Pilgrims to New England in 1620 and taught them to survive in the woodland. Forty years later, many more English had come, and the Pequamid were being driven from their homes.

Up and down the Atlantic Coast, Europeans forced Native Americans off their land, sometimes violently. By 1776, when Thomas Jefferson wrote the Declaration of Independence, most of the East Coast tribes had been wiped out or pushed west.

"Where are the Narragansett, the Mohican, the Pokanoket, and many other powerful tribes of our people?" asked the Shawnee chief Tecumseh. They have vanished before the white settlers, Tecumseh concluded, "as snow before a summer sun."

In 1803, Jefferson was President of the United States. Hoping to enlarge his young nation, Jefferson acquired a vast piece of land west of the Mississippi River. The United States bought this land, known as the Louisiana Purchase, from France.

Jefferson sent out two explorers, Meriwether Lewis and William Clark, to map the new territory and describe any new animals and plants they found. Lewis and Clark wrote that they had seen "one of the fairest portions of the globe."

Lewis and Clark's lush descriptions inspired many people to move west. Americans cleared forests and built towns all the way to the Mississippi River. They followed trails leading farther west.

The west promised many things to many people. To some, it gave hope of a new life and new opportunities. These easterners packed their belongings into wagons and set out to try their luck on the frontier.

Some sought a place where they could worship freely. The members of a new religion, the Church of Jesus Christ of Latter-Day Saints, had been driven from many eastern towns. These people, known as the Mormons, founded a settlement in the wilderness, called Salt Lake City, in 1847.

The desire for wealth lured many people. In 1848, a carpenter named John Marshall discovered gold in California's American River. Soon, prospectors were traveling west in the California Gold Rush, to search the mountains and streambeds for gold of their own.

The west promised opportunities to African Americans, too. Following the Civil War, thousands of black people became pioneers. Black farmers, laborers, and their families settled in Kansas, Texas, and other western states. By 1900, 766,000 African Americans made their homes in the west.

The end of the Civil War also brought the rumble and smoke of railroads. Workers for the Central Pacific Railroad began laying tracks in Sacramento, California, and moved east. The Union Pacific Railroad started in the east and went west.

The two lines of track met at Promontory Point, Utah, in May 1869, and were joined with

A free black man, working as a miner in the west.

a golden spike. "May God continue the unity of our Country," read the inscription on the spike, "as this Railroad united the two great Oceans of the world."

And while the United States was creating "unity," what happened to the Indians? In the early 1800s, as settlers moved beyond the Appalachian Mountains, the government adopted a policy of "Indian removal." The government uprooted tribes and forced them to find homes on the Great Plains. There, the government promised, Native Americans could live in peace "as long as trees grow and the waters run." It was one of many promises that soon would be broken.

Some Indians fought to hold onto their land. In 1831, the Sac and Fox tribes tried to reclaim their land in Illinois. Months of fighting resulted. The battle ended in 1832, when the Sac and Fox met the fate of many Native Americans who resisted being moved. Soldiers killed most of their fighting men.

The journey to new land was often long and difficult. In 1838, the government forced the Cherokee people to leave their homes in the southeast. As many as eighteen thousand Cherokees were forced to march to the Great Plains along a route they called the "Trail of Tears."

More than four thousand Cherokees died from disease, exhaustion, or exposure to the winter weather before they reached their new home in the Indian Territory. The Cherokee people who survived came to a land that was already occupied. The Indian Territory was the home of nomadic tribes such as the Kiowa and Comanche.

The Indians of the Great Plains resented the Cherokees and other incoming tribes. But even more, they resented the white settlers who built ranches and railroad tracks on their hunting grounds. It angered the Native Americans to see settlers shoot buffalo for sport. The Plains tribes depended on buffalo meat for food and buffalo skins for shelter and warm clothing.

The Plains Indians fought back in the only ways that they could. They attacked the newly arrived eastern tribes. They also attacked the wagon trains that brought more settlers to the west. They tore up the railroad tracks that cut paths across the grassland.

"The Great Spirit raised both the white man and the Indian," said Red Cloud, a chief of the powerful Sioux people. "I think he raised the Indian first. He raised me in this land and it belongs to me."

Red Cloud, a Sioux chief

Chapter 4

War on the Plains

On August 1, 1867, a call for help reached Fort Hays, Kansas. There had been a fight between workers and Cheyenne Indians at a railroad camp. At least seven people were dead. The workers hoped the Army could prevent another fight.

Early the next morning, Captain George Armes and thirty-four soldiers of the 10th Cavalry saddled their horses and headed for the camp. Suddenly, a group of armed Cheyennes surrounded the troop. A gunfight broke out between the Cheyennes, who were crouched behind rocks and shrubs, and the soldiers, trapped in the center.

After six hours of fighting, the soldiers were running out of bullets. They had to break through the circle of Cheyennes to escape. The cavalrymen readied their rifles. And when Captain Armes gave the order, they shot their way through.

It was a dangerous maneuver, but it worked. Every soldier but one escaped. Sergeant William

Christy, the Pennsylvania farmer, was shot in the head. He became the first member of the 10th Cavalry to die in battle.

With deeds such as this, the African-American soldiers soon earned a reputation for courage. The native people began to call them Buffalo Soldiers.

There are several stories to explain this nickname. According to one story, the soldiers wore thick, furry buffalo hides in winter. All wrapped up, with their dark skin and curly hair, they reminded the Indians of buffaloes. Another story says that the Native Americans admired the soldiers' bravery, just as they admired the strong and plentiful buffalo.

The Buffalo Soldiers accepted their new name with pride. The 10th Cavalry even included a buffalo in its regimental crest, or emblem. And the black cavalrymen continued to risk their lives in the service of their country.

In April 1870, 9th Cavalry troops set out from Fort McKavett, Texas. They were looking for some Apache Indians who had been in fights with settlers. The soldiers searched the plains for weeks. Their clothing ripped, and their boots fell apart. At last they found the Apaches—and quickly saw that they were outnumbered.

The Apaches were armed with rifles, and they approached the soldiers from behind. Cap-

The regimental crest of the 10th Cavalry

tain Henry Carroll, the officer in charge, ordered the soldiers to turn around and ride toward the Indians.

Riding into the face of an enemy meant risking death, but Emanuel Stance of South Carolina was willing to take that risk. Stance led a group of soldiers forward and ordered them to fire. This strong show of courage convinced the Apaches to retreat.

Stance received the Congressional Medal of Honor for his actions. He was the first of twenty 9th and 10th cavalrymen—seventeen black soldiers and three white officers—to win the Medal of Honor. "I will cherish the gift as a thing of priceless value," he wrote, "and endeavor by my future conduct to merit the high honor conferred upon me."

Most soldiers in the Indian Wars received few rewards or thanks. "Of all warfare," wrote Major Guy Henry, a white officer with the 9th Cavalry, service in the Indian Wars was "the most dangerous, the most trying and the most thankless."

The fighting was dangerous, Henry explained, "because your foe is behind cover." The Native Americans knew the terrain well, so they knew the best places to seek protection.

It was trying, or difficult, for several reasons. "You are on reduced rations, exposed to intense cold, fires often being forbidden; if wounded, there is no transportation or possible care."

The fighting was thankless, Henry stated, because "the sense of duty performed in defense of the weak settler is your only reward."

The black cavalrymen fought more than sixty frontier battles. One of their most dangerous, trying, and thankless campaigns was the hunt for Victorio, the man known as the Apache Wolf. Chief Victorio was a forceful leader, and a skilled and fearless fighting man.

By 1875, most of the Apaches had moved to reservations—areas set aside by the government for their use. At first the Apaches dwelled on reservations with mountains and trees, on land where they had lived for centuries. But in 1876, the government moved all of the Apaches to the San Carlos Reservation in Arizona. The Apaches hated that dry, barren place.

In September 1877, Victorio and a band of three hundred Apaches fled San Carlos. They roamed the countryside, getting into fights with ranchers. The government called for Victorio's capture, dead or alive. General John Pope ordered the 9th Cavalry to do the job.

By October, Colonel Hatch's soldiers had chased Victorio's band into the mountains and forced them to surrender. But when the time came to return to San Carlos, Victorio and eighty others escaped again. Victorio swore that he would rather die than submit to the United States government.

Hatch and his men spent months pursuing Victorio over the rough, rocky terrain. "The work performed by these troops is most arduous, horses worn to mere shadows, men nearly without boots, shoes and clothing," Hatch noted. "Long night

Victorio, known as the Apache Wolf

marches have been made on foot by these troops in their efforts to surprise the Indian camp."

Often it seemed that the soldiers nearly had Victorio in their grasp—and then he seemed to vanish into the hills and canyons.

Victorio moved south to Mexico, where the U.S. Army could not follow. There, Victorio vowed "to make war forever." When he and his followers killed twenty-six Mexican citizens, the Mexican Army joined the fight. The Mexican soldiers chased Victorio back to the United States.

On the evening of May 13, 1880, Buffalo Soldier George Jordan, and twenty-five others from the 9th Cavalry, arrived at a New Mexico stagecoach station. They were on their way to Tularosa, a small settlement built near an old fort. Victorio was headed for Tularosa, too, but the soldiers expected to arrive first.

"We were all ready for a good night's rest," Jordan recalled. But then a messenger arrived. Victorio was very close to Tularosa, the messenger warned. The Buffalo Soldiers rode all night to reach Tularosa. As they approached the town, the citizens hurried out to greet them. "They came out of their houses waving towels and handkerchiefs for joy," Jordan reported.

Victorio had not yet arrived, the citizens said. They urged the soldiers to go out and attack the

Apaches. "I could not do this," Jordan explained. "My orders were to protect the people in the town."

Wasting no time, Jordan ordered some of the soldiers to build a stockade, a barrier made of fence posts. Jordan related what happened next: "As the Indians' rifles began to crack the people rushed to the fort and stockade." Again and again, the Apaches tried to enter the stockade. "But we repulsed them each time," Jordan said.

The soldiers' quick action saved many lives. It caused Victorio's band to give up and leave the region. "Our little detachment was somewhat of a surprise to the Indians," Jordan concluded. George Jordan received the Congressional Medal of Honor for his bravery and quick thinking.

Soldiers of the 10th Cavalry in camp during the Apache Wars

Victorio's army of Apaches turned up next in Texas, where the 10th Cavalry was now quartered. Colonel Grierson stationed soldiers at many watering holes and mountain passes—places where Victorio was sure to turn up.

On August 6, 1880, Victorio and his followers came to a spot called Rattlesnake Canyon, looking for water. Grierson's soldiers met them with gunfire, and the Apaches scattered.

The soldiers and Indians met again five days later. This time, the 10th Cavalry killed or wounded more than thirty Apaches and took many of their animals. They chased the survivors into Mexico.

Victorio never returned to the United States. On October 14, the Mexican Army surrounded his band in some hills near the town of Chihuahua. The Mexicans killed Victorio and most of his followers.

The Mexicans took credit for Victorio's defeat, but they owed their success to the Buffalo Soldiers. General E. O. C. Ord, head of the Army's forces in Texas, praised the "earnest and zealous efforts" of the Buffalo Soldiers.

By June 1885, most Native Americans were living on reservations. Towns were springing up across the West. While the 10th Cavalry remained in the southwest, bringing the Apache Wars to an end, the 9th Cavalry moved to the northern plains.

For years, white regiments on the northern plains had fought against the Sioux, powerful tribes of hunters and warriors who followed the buffalo herds. The struggle had been fierce, with many deaths on both sides.

The most famous battle took place in present-day Montana in 1876, when the 7th Cavalry marched through an Indian camp beside the Little Bighorn River.

The soldier in the lead was easily recognized. He was fair-skinned, red-headed General George Custer, the man the Native Americans called Long Hair. Custer, who years earlier had refused to serve with black troops, had gained fame as an Indian fighter.

The Indian women and children fled as the cavalry marched through their camp. The soldiers did not know, however, that hundreds of Sioux and Cheyenne men were waiting in a ravine, armed with rifles and mounted on their horses.

As the soldiers neared the ravine, the Indian men rode out and surprised them—"like bees swarming out of a hive," said Kill Eagle, a Sioux chief. The fight that took place was swift and violent. "The Sioux shot straight, and the soldiers fell dead," said one Sioux woman. "Long Hair lay

dead among the rest."

By the time the 9th Cavalry arrived on the northern plains, the Sioux had been rounded up onto reservations in North Dakota and South Dakota. The fighting seemed to be over.

But the Sioux people longed for their old way of life, and a new religion offered them hope. The "Ghost Dance Religion" taught that new soil would soon cover the earth and bury the white people. The ghost of every Indian who died in battle would return, and many buffalo would once more graze on the plains. The believers preached that those

General George Custer met his death at the Battle of Little Big Horn.

who performed the "ghost dance" would be part of the renewed world.

On every reservation, the Sioux danced and grew impatient for change. Their behavior alarmed the white Americans, who feared the Sioux were preparing for war. "Indians are dancing in the snow and are wild and crazy," reported a government official. "We need protection, and we need it now."

Army leaders blamed the Sioux chief Sitting Bull for stirring up trouble. Older than the other Sioux chiefs, Sitting Bull was greatly respected by his people. He was courageous and sure of himself, and refused to submit to the U.S. government. "If the Great Spirit has chosen anyone to be the chief of this country," he stated, "it is myself."

On December 15, 1890, law-enforcement officers came to arrest Sitting Bull. A fight broke out between the officers and Sitting Bull's followers, and bullets flew through the air. One struck Sitting Bull in the head, and he died. Frightened, the chief's followers fled to the Badlands, a rough, rocky region.

Ninth Cavalry troops searched for the hidden bands of Sioux. It was a hard, unpleasant mission. Buffalo Soldier Charles Creek recalled sleeping "out in the cold like a dog, not in a tent because the Indians gonna sneak up on you." Said Creek, "It was so cold the spit froze when it left your

Sitting Bull

mouth."

Meanwhile soldiers of the 7th Cavalry rounded up 350 Sioux. The soldiers and Indians camped beside a creek called Wounded Knee. The Sioux families spent the night in tepees and Army tents.

The next morning, the soldiers called the Sioux men together and told them to give up their guns. "All of us gave the guns and they were stacked up in the center," said a man named White Lance.

The soldiers suspected that some Native Americans were hiding rifles, though, and began to rummage through their tents. Suddenly, a young man named Black Coyote appeared with a rifle held over his head. It was an expensive, new weapon that he did not want to surrender.

As the soldiers wrestled it from him, a gunshot echoed across the camp. It was as loud as a "lightning crash," one Sioux recalled. That single gunshot caused the soldiers to panic. They began shooting wildly, striking men, women, and children.

A painting, artist unknown, of the massacre at Wounded Knee

"We tried to run, but they shot us like buffalo," said Louise Weasel Bear, a Sioux woman. When the shooting stopped, more than three hundred Sioux lay dead or dying on the cold ground.

News of the killings spread across the Badlands. Determined to get even, Sioux riflemen took up posts on the walls of a narrow canyon. They waited for the 7th Cavalry to ride through, then they opened fire.

Nearby, the Buffalo Soldiers were trying to get some sleep after days of riding in the freezing weather. But when they heard the gunfire, they mounted their horses and came to the 7th Cavalry's aid. They split up and attacked the Sioux from the east and west, and managed to drive them off.

That was the last time the Native Americans tried to fight for their land and for their way of life. Over the next few weeks, they gave up the battle and returned to the reservations.

Today the massacre at Wounded Knee is remembered as the event that ended the Indian Wars. "A people's dream died there," recalled Black Elk of the Sioux people. "It was a beautiful dream."

Chapter 5

Just and Peaceable Men

The Buffalo Soldiers belonged to a race of people who also had a dream. America's black citizens longed for the same treatment and opportunities as whites.

In the years following the Civil War, Americans made important additions to the Constitution. The Constitution now outlawed slavery. It gave all citizens protection under the law, and guaranteed black men the right to vote.

However, African Americans still faced many obstacles. Southern states passed laws called "black codes," which restricted black people's freedom. For example, an African American who married a white person would be sent to prison. Mississippi had a law against black people owning farmland.

Governor B. F. Perry of South Carolina expressed the thoughts of most southern leaders. His state had a "white man's government," Perry said, "intended for white men only."

African Americans were forbidden to handle guns in some southern towns. In many places, they had to be off the streets at night. Bands of whites roamed the countryside, terrorizing black citizens and setting fire to black children's schools.

The black population enjoyed more freedom in the north. But even there, blacks were denied good jobs and kept out of white society. They lived in separate neighborhoods, worshiped in separate churches, and learned in separate schools.

In the West, the Buffalo Soldiers endured unfair—and often cruel—treatment because of their race.

In 1870, a white settler shot and killed Private Boston Henry of the 9th Cavalry, who was stationed at Fort McKavett, Texas. The murderer fled to escape capture, and later killed two of the Buffalo Soldiers who pursued him. When the settler was at last captured and brought to trial, a white jury declared him not guilty.

Racism claimed another soldier's life on the night of January 31, 1881. Private William Watkins of the 10th Cavalry was out having fun that night, singing and dancing in a San Angelo, Texas, saloon. A white rancher named Tom McCarthy was enjoying Watkins's songs and told him to continue. When Watkins protested that he was tired, McCarthy shot the soldier in the head.

The sheriff considered it a minor crime to kill an African American. He let McCarthy go free until his trial. When they learned of this, some of the Buffalo Soldiers handed out a notice in San Angelo. It read: "We, the soldiers of the U.S. Army do hereby warn the first and last time all citizens, cowboys, etc., of San Angelo and vicinity to recognize our right of way as just and peaceable men."

That summer, a jury in Austin, Texas, decided that McCarthy was not guilty. The soldiers were furious. Anxious to avoid trouble between the cavalry and townspeople, Grierson confined the soldiers to Fort Concho all summer.

African Americans also faced great obstacles as they struggled to gain opportunities in the armed forces. In 1877, Lieutenant Henry Flipper became the first African American to graduate from the United States Military Academy at West Point, a school that trains young people for careers as Army officers.

In 1878, Flipper headed west to serve with the 10th Cavalry. Henry Flipper, a black officer, was going to command troops.

The new lieutenant quickly proved himself to be a smart and capable officer. At Fort Sill, in Indian Territory, he designed a system for draining stagnant pools of water. The water had been a breeding place

for disease-carrying mosquitoes.

Flipper also showed strength and bravery in the field. He once rode his horse for twenty-two hours to warn Colonel Grierson that Victorio's band was near.

Soon after his arrival in the West, Flipper made friends with a young white woman named Molly Dwyer. The two often went riding together. Some white officers disapproved of this friendship between a white woman and a black man.

Following Victorio's capture, the Army transferred Lieutenant Flipper to Fort Davis, Texas. The commander at Fort Davis, Colonel William Shafter, disliked the African-American officer. Other whites at Fort Davis resented him, too. It bothered them that Flipper had achieved an officer's status. They had heard about his friendship with Molly Dwyer, and this angered them as well.

Colonel Shafter placed Flipper in charge of the commissary, or store, at the fort. Flipper also took care of the commissary funds. He worked hard to be a model officer. "Never did a man walk the path of uprightness straighter than I did," Flipper wrote. He knew the other officers were watching him closely. If he made just one mistake, they would see it as proof that blacks made poor officers.

In spite of his efforts, Flipper discovered, in July 1881, that commissary funds were missing

Lieutenant Henry Flipper

"The question before you is whether it is possible for a colored man to secure and hold a position as an officer in the Army."

from his trunk. He kept quiet about the loss. Flipper knew that if he reported it to Shafter, he would be blamed. He decided to make up the loss from his own money, little by little.

Shafter soon learned about the missing funds, though, and had Flipper arrested. Shafter charged Flipper with stealing, a crime that was considered "conduct unbecoming an officer."

Flipper believed that he was the victim of a cruel trick. He suspected that the other officers had taken the money to make him look bad.

Henry Flipper paid back the missing money within two weeks. If he had been white, say some historians, the matter would have ended then. But Flipper was tried in a court-martial, a hearing to determine whether he had broken any military laws.

Henry Flipper's lawyer believed that the trial was about more than missing commissary funds. "The question before you," Flipper's lawyer told the court, "is whether it is possible for a colored man to secure and hold a position as an officer in the Army."

The verdict showed that the lawyer was right. The members of the court found Flipper innocent of stealing the money. For the charge of conduct unbecoming an officer, however, the verdict was guilty. The court had found a way to get Henry

Flipper out of the Army. The black lieutenant received a dishonorable discharge, which would remain as a shameful mark on his record.

Henry Flipper went on to work as a surveyor, a mining engineer, an author, and a newspaper editor. He served as an aide to a U.S. senator and helped to develop Alaska's railway system. Nine times, he tried to get Congress to remove the dishonorable discharge from his record, but nine times he failed. In spite of his achievements, Henry Flipper died, in 1940, a disappointed man.

Fort Sill, Indian Territory, Lt. Flipper's first post

45

Chapter 6

Hardships, Outlaws, and Boomers

The Buffalo Soldiers lived a hard, lonely life on the frontier. Most western forts were nothing more than clusters of run-down shacks, far from towns and entertainment.

Frontier soldiers—black and white—slept in crowded barracks without bathtubs or showers. When General M. C. Meigs inspected some Texas forts in 1869, he was "horrified," he said, to see "the roughboard, vermin-infested bunks in which the men slept."

The unclean conditions led to a high rate of disease. Colds and diarrhea spread rapidly through the ranks. Tuberculosis, an illness that attacked the lungs, claimed many lives. More frontier soldiers died from disease than from fighting in the Indian Wars.

The Buffalo Soldiers put in long, tiring days at their forts. They awoke at 5:20 AM to the sound of a trumpeter playing reveille. Twenty minutes later, they hurried to the stables to feed their horses. After breakfast at 6:40, they spent the day on guard duty, practicing military drills, and grooming and exercising their horses.

The soldiers ate dinner promptly at 12:30 PM. Just as the black soldiers received poorer horses and equipment than white regiments, they often ate inferior food. The post surgeon at Fort Concho, New Mexico, reported that the black cavalrymen stationed there ate poor-quality meat and bad-tasting canned peas. Their bread was often sour.

The Buffalo Soldiers kept busy even after sundown. Some had never learned to read or write, and so took nightly lessons from the regiment's chaplain.

At Fort Davis, Texas, in 1877, the Buffalo Soldiers marched in a dress parade every evening, except Saturday. The soldiers marched in full uniform while the post band played. All watched as the American flag was lowered for the night.

Although they took pride in their uniforms, the Buffalo Soldiers dressed for comfort in the field. "Most of the men ride in their blue flannel shirts," observed a white lieutenant who saw the

Fort Davis, Texas

black cavalry on patrol in Arizona. "Some of the men take off their shirts and ride in their gray knit undershirts. There are all sorts of hats worn, American and Mexican make, the most common being the ugly army campaign hat of gray felt."

The soldiers' clothing also showed the effects of weeks spent on the trail. "There are few trousers not torn or badly worn," the lieutenant wrote, "especially in the seat."

The Buffalo Soldiers seldom complained, however. A newspaper reporter who visited Fort Sill in Indian Territory found the black soldiers to be "active, intelligent, and resolute men."

"These 'buffalo soldiers,'" observed the reporter, "appear to me to be rather superior to the average white men recruited in time of peace. Their officers explain this by saying that the best colored young men can be recruited in time of peace."

A dress parade of the 9th Cavalry at Fort Davis

Only "indifferent or inferior whites" wish to enlist during peacetime, the reporter said.

The Buffalo Soldiers needed all of their intelligence and strength to survive in an environment with hot and cold temperatures, wild animals, narrow mountain passes, and vast deserts. They patrolled in places that had never been mapped—and unknown territory presented special risks.

In the summer of 1877, forty 10th Cavalry soldiers were scouting the Texas plains. Their journey brought them into a region where they had never been. They had a Mexican guide, though, and he claimed to know the area.

The soldiers sipped at the water in their canteens, trying to make it last. After two or three days without water, they knew, a person can die. But in the dry heat and constant sun, the water soon was gone.

The guide kept promising a watering hole was nearby, but he never could find it. At last, afraid to admit that he was lost, the guide ran off. He abandoned the Buffalo Soldiers in the desert.

The soldiers were so hot and thirsty that some grew dizzy and fainted. The weakest ones fell behind. By the third day, Lieutenant Charles Cooper, one of the officers in charge, noted "their tongues and throats were swollen, and they were unable even to swallow their saliva—in fact, they had no

saliva to swallow."

Exhausted, thirsty horses collapsed and died. Cooper ordered the men to slit the throats of the dead horses and drink their blood to survive.

"The fourth day without water was dreadful," Cooper said. He recalled "men gasping in death around us; horses falling dead to the right and left; the crazed survivors of our men fighting his neighbor for the blood of horses."

At last, the soldiers spotted Double Lakes, a

A Frederic Remington drawing titled "A Pull at the Canteen"

place they recognized. They drank deeply and filled their canteens. They carried water to the men who had fallen behind. Most of the soldiers lived to return to their fort. Only four men were lost.

This region, where soldiers could wander unseen for days, was also a place where outlaws could hide. The wide, open west attracted drifters and lawbreakers from the east, who preyed upon the isolated towns. Frontier settlers hired sheriffs to protect them, but many sheriffs died in gunfights, or turned out to be crooked themselves. Westerners often called upon the Army for protection.

At times, the Buffalo Soldiers answered these calls. They brought order and safety to towns such as Lincoln, New Mexico, which was known as a lawless place in the 1870s.

Two groups of wealthy businessmen were fighting to control Lincoln's bank and general store. Each group hired gunmen to fight for its interests. One hired gunman was a slim young man known as Billy the Kid. By the time he was nineteen years old, Billy boasted about killing twenty-one people.

Gun battles broke out on Lincoln's streets, and people could not walk safely in town. In February 1878, the governor of New Mexico asked the Army for help.

From Fort Concho, where the 9th Cavalry was

stationed, Colonel Hatch sent Captain George Purington and twenty-five soldiers to Lincoln. But the men quickly saw that their force was too small to stop all of the fighting. The best they could do, the soldiers realized, was to protect the honest citizens of Lincoln. Purington told the feuding men that if they must fight, they should "withdraw to the mountains and fight to their hearts' content." The soldiers then returned to their fort.

The fighting did not remain in the mountains, though. On April 1, Lincoln's sheriff and two deputies were shot and killed while walking down the street. Soon, the time came for a showdown.

On July 14, two armies of outlaws—nearly one hundred men—rode into Lincoln. They took positions in houses and stores. For four days, the sound of gunfire filled the air. Outlaws fell, killed or wounded. The gunfight did not end until one of the feuding businessmen lay dead and his home had been burned to the ground.

Weeks of looting and lawlessness followed, as Billy the Kid and his companions roamed the streets. At last the President of the United States called for calm. He ordered the Army back to Lincoln.

The Buffalo Soldiers spent months tracking down the outlaws, but they did not capture Billy the Kid. He was trapped and killed by a western sheriff. Still, the 9th Cavalry helped to bring law and order to Lincoln—and they received little thanks.

Many of Lincoln's citizens spoke with hatred of African Americans and insulted the black soldiers. "Unquestionably," said Colonel Hatch, "the troops find this duty disagreeable."

The 9th Cavalry performed another unpleasant duty during the 1880s. White settlers were moving into a section of the Indian Territory. This section was called the "Unassigned Lands," because it had not been assigned to any tribe. It was against the law for Americans to live and farm there, so the Buffalo Soldiers had to move the settlers out.

These settlers were deliberately breaking the law. Called "Boomers," they wanted to create a "boom," or rapid growth of building and profits. The Boomers tried to force the government to allow settlement of the Unassigned Lands. They defiantly built houses and schools there, and began to farm.

Moving the Boomers out was a thankless task, because most Americans were in favor of the Boomers' activities. And once they had moved out, the Boomers often returned to the Unassigned Lands, settling in other places. There was always the danger of bloodshed as well. Many Boomers wanted to fight rather than to cooperate with the

Army.

The Buffalo Soldiers disliked using force to make people obey the law, but sometimes they had no choice. In August 1882, when a group of Boomers refused to leave, the Buffalo Soldiers tied up their hands and feet. The soldiers tossed the Boomers into their wagons "as if they were sacks of corn," noted one observer.

In 1884, the soldiers discovered 1,500 Boomers living at a place called Rock Falls. Colonel Hatch ordered the settlers to leave. If they stayed, the Army would drive them out, Hatch warned.

Most of the Boomers packed up their belongings and left, but two hundred fifty of them refused to budge. The soldiers had to remove them by force. And to make sure that no one returned, they set fire to the settlers' houses and barns.

Six months later, the 9th Cavalry located three hundred Boomers camped beside Stillwater Creek. Their leader told Hatch the Boomers would rather fight than leave. Hatch hoped to avoid a battle that could result in the deaths of settlers and soldiers, so he came up with a plan to make the Boomers leave peacefully.

Hatch posted soldiers around the settlement and ordered them to stop any wagons carrying food. With no new provisions getting through, the Boomers used up their food supply. After five days, the hungry settlers decided to leave.

The 9th Cavalry put in years of hard work on the Unassigned Lands, but it was work that came to nothing. On March 23, 1893, President Benjamin Harrison announced that the Unassigned Lands would open to settlers on April 22. More than 50,000 people lined up on the Oklahoma border that day, ready to rush into the territory and claim a plot of land.

The Oklahoma Land Rush was like nothing the nation had ever seen. Within days, the settlers had set up tents, shacks, and storefronts on the once open land. The days of the "Wild West" were over. The director of the U.S. Census, in Washington, D.C., announced that the frontier no longer existed.

The Buffalo Soldiers had witnessed great changes during more than twenty-five years on the frontier. They had seen the Native Americans defeated and forced onto reservations. They had seen ranches, towns, and cities grow where buffalo once grazed.

The soldiers had seen men come and go during their long years of service as well. Many of the men who had enlisted back in 1866 had retired or died. Colonel Hatch died at Fort Robinson, Nebraska, in April 1889.

Colonel Grierson passed the command of the 10th Cavalry on to a younger officer in 1888. "The officers and enlisted men have cheerfully endured many hardships and privations," Colonel Grierson said on that occasion, "and in the midst of great dangers steadfastly maintained a most gallant and zealous devotion to duty, and they may well be proud of the record made."

A formation of the 9th Cavalry at Fort Robinson, Nebraska

Chapter 7

Fighting on Foreign Soil

With pride in their achievements, the Buffalo Soldiers remained ready to go wherever their nation needed them. In 1898, they were called to serve in Cuba. This tropical island sits at the entrance to the Gulf of Mexico, just ninety miles south of Florida.

Since 1511, Cuba had been a colony belonging to Spain. But in the 1890s, Cuba was struggling to become an independent nation. The Cubans resented their Spanish rulers, claiming they were unjust and cruel.

Some American newspapers stirred up the public's interest in the Cuban fight for independence. They printed sensational stories about Cubans who were dead, sick, or starving, due to Spanish brutality. One newspaper called the struggle, so close to America's shore, "blood on the doorstep." The newspapers urged their country to get involved.

Americans watched the events in Cuba for another reason as well. The world now recognized the United States as the most powerful nation in the Western Hemisphere. Many Americans disliked the fact that Spain, a European country, had control over land and people in the Americas.

The United States sent a battleship, the U.S.S. *Maine*, to Havana Harbor in Cuba. The *Maine* was on a "friendly visit," government officials said. However, they hoped the presence of a U.S. ship would show American concern for the future of Cuba. The government had a practical reason for sending the *Maine* as well. The Navy could evacuate Americans from Cuba on the *Maine* if heavy fighting broke out.

Havana Harbor was quiet on the night of February 15, 1898. At 9:40 PM, without warning, a huge explosion tore apart the *Maine*. The ship sank, killing two hundred sixty crew members, including twenty-two African Americans. (The Navy permitted black and white enlisted men to serve together.)

Many people blamed Spain for the blast, although no one knew its true cause. And by April, the United States and Spain were at war. "Remember the *Maine*!" Americans cried, as their nation prepared for battle.

The government called upon its peacetime forces, including the four black regiments, to fight in the Spanish-American War. For the first time, African Americans would fight for their country in a foreign land.

The Buffalo Soldiers traveled by train from the northern plains to Tampa, Florida, where they would board ships bound for Cuba. In the hurry, the government had not issued lightweight uniforms to the black troops. They had only heavy wool uniforms to wear. Warm and practical in the North, these uniforms would be hot and uncomfortable in tropical Cuba.

The 9th Cavalry boarding trains bound for Tampa, Florida.

As they passed through towns in Minnesota, the soldiers saw railroad stations decorated with flags and flowers in their honor. But as they traveled south, they saw fewer and fewer decorations. In one town where they stopped, the barber hung up a sign warning African Americans to keep out of his shop.

Such prejudice prompted George Prioleau, the 9th Cavalry's chaplain, to write an angry letter to a northern newspaper. "The Negro of this country is a free man and yet a slave," wrote Prioleau. "He sings 'My Country 'Tis of Thee, Sweet Land of Liberty,' and though the word 'liberty' chokes him, he swallows it and finishes the stanza 'of Thee I Sing.'"

When the African-American cavalrymen arrived in Tampa, they saw many American soldiers waiting to board ships. They saw the 24th and 25th Infantry, the black foot soldiers. They also saw the Rough Riders, a group of cowboys, adventurers, and wealthy young men who knew little about fighting wars. Their leader was a jaunty fellow, Colonel Theodore Roosevelt, who would be President of the United States one day.

The soldiers boarded ships, along with their supplies, horses, and mules. On June 22, they arrived in Cuba. The ships docked offshore at a spot where the winds created high waves.

"The Negro of this country is a free man and yet a slave."

61

The 9th Cavalry preparing to board ship and sail to Cuba.

One at a time, the soldiers climbed through portholes and dropped fifteen feet to the steam-powered boats that would bring them to shore. Jumping empty-handed would have been hard enough, but each soldier carried a heavy load of gear—his rifle, ammunition, blanket roll, tent, poncho, and enough food to last three days.

One day after they arrived, the cavalry regiments moved inland. They joined a force headed for a gap in the hills named Las Guasimas. The men traveled slowly along the overgrown jungle paths. "At times there was hardly room for more than a single file," one soldier said.

At Las Guasimas, the 10th Cavalry came to the Rough Riders' aid. While making their way through jungle trees, Roosevelt's men had come under heavy gunfire from Spanish sharpshooters. They could not fight their way out, because they could not find their machine guns. The guns were "mislaid," said Stephen Bonal, a newspaperman who saw the battle. "At least the mules carrying them could not be found."

Using skills they had learned in the Indian Wars, the Buffalo Soldiers rescued the Rough Riders. They passed the Rough Riders to the right and left and quickly defeated the Spaniards. One white officer admitted that without help from the Buffalo Soldiers, "the Rough Riders would have been exterminated."

"I never saw such fighting as those 10th Cavalry did," said another white soldier. "They didn't seem to know what fear was."

Private Augustus Wally of the 9th Cavalry became a hero at the Battle of Las Guasimas. Wally noticed that an officer had been shot in the leg and could not walk. As bullets flew around him, Wally ran to the wounded officer and carried him to safety. Wally's actions earned him the Congressional Medal of Honor.

On July 1, the Buffalo Soldiers helped the Americans win the most important battle of the Spanish-American War. The battle took place on Kettle Hill and on San Juan Hill, outside the city of Santiago. The American generals considered the hills to be a key position. They ordered their forces to capture them from the Spanish.

To reach the hills, the American soldiers had to crawl through dense jungle growth while the Spanish fired at them. Sergeant Thomas Griffith of the 10th Cavalry crawled ahead of the others. He cut away the barbed wire that the Spanish had twisted around bushes and trees.

The battle began at 2 PM. The soldiers left the safety of their jungle covering. Traveling on foot, the 9th Cavalry and the Rough Riders headed toward Kettle Hill, while the 10th Cavalry set out for San Juan Hill.

Again, the battle-hardened Buffalo Soldiers defeated the Spanish gunmen. "When a soldier put up his head to fire, sometimes as many as six of our bullets would strike his head at once," said Sergeant R. Anderson, a black soldier. "This action on our part wholly destroyed the discipline of the enemy so that they would not show any part of their body, but would simply stick their rifles above their entrenchments and fire without aim."

Lieutenant John J. Pershing, a young white officer serving with the 10th Cavalry, described what he saw. "White regiments, black regiments, regulars and Rough Riders, representing the young manhood of the North and South, fought shoulder to shoulder," Pershing recalled. All of the soldiers, noted Pershing, were "mindful only of the common duty as Americans."

By sunset, the Americans had won the battle. "It was glorious," Pershing said. "For the moment every thought was forgotten but victory. We officers of the 10th Cavalry could have taken our black heroes in our arms."

Everyone present knew who was responsible for the victory. "The negroes saved that fight,"

Soldiers, black and white, carry the wounded from the fighting near Santiago.

"The services of no four white regiments can be compared to those rendered by the four colored regiments—the 9th and 10th Cavalry and the 24th and 25th Infantry."

said one white veteran of the battle. Another added, "The services of no four white regiments can be compared to those rendered by the four colored regiments—the 9th and 10th Cavalry and the 24th and 25th Infantry."

More than one thousand Americans died in the famous battle. The Buffalo Soldiers' losses were especially high. One of every five black soldiers lost his life. And more than half of the 10th Cavalry's officers died.

On July 3, the United States Navy destroyed the Spanish naval squadron in Santiago's harbor. Two weeks later, Spain sought peace with the United States. The Spanish-American War was over. Cuba was an independent nation, and the victorious Americans returned home.

The Buffalo Soldiers and Rough Riders docked at Montauk Point, Long Island, in August. The American people cheered the Rough Riders as heroes. The public largely ignored the returning African Americans, though. "These black boys, heroes of our country, were not allowed to stand at the counters of the restaurants and drink a cup of coffee," wrote the chaplain, George Prioleau. "The white soldiers were welcomed and invited to sit down at the tables and eat free of cost."

Prioleau lamented, "It seems as if God has forgotten us."

Chapter 8

True Patriots

John J. Pershing never forgot the Buffalo Soldiers' fine service in Cuba. In 1916, Pershing requested that the 10th Cavalry accompany him to Mexico.

President Woodrow Wilson had asked Pershing, who was now a general, to lead a campaign in Mexico. Wilson wanted Pershing to capture Pancho Villa, a man who hoped to seize power in that country. Villa and his followers had murdered some American mining engineers. They had crossed the border to attack American towns.

The 10th Cavalry embarked on its toughest mission. For a year, the men rode their horses for hundreds of miles over the rutted Mexican landscape.

The days were hot, and the nights were cold. The soldiers had no coats, and the water froze in their canteens. Horses grew weak and died. Food was scarce, and supplies were low. The cavalrymen used leather from their saddles to repair their worn-out boots.

John J. Pershing was nicknamed "Black Jack" after his service with the Buffalo Soldiers.

Finding Pancho Villa was like "trying to catch a rat in a cornfield," Pershing said. Villa always seemed to stay ahead of the Army and avoid capture. Sometimes the soldiers missed him by hours.

The search for Pancho Villa turned out to be a fruitless, thankless job. America's leaders soon lost interest in the campaign. They focused their attention instead on the war then raging in Europe, World War I. England, France, and other countries were at war with Germany.

The Army returned from Mexico, and the United States entered the war overseas. Pershing went on to command the American forces in Europe. About his service with the Buffalo Soldiers, Pershing said, "It has been an honor which I am proud to claim."

During World War I, the Army began to train black officers to serve with black regiments. Army leaders still would not allow black officers to command white troops.

Although black cavalry soldiers did not serve in World War I, the 92nd Infantry, another black regiment, carried on in the Buffalo Soldier tradition. Its members were among the 200,000 African Americans who served in that war, from 1917 to 1919. Forty-three of the regiment's soldiers and fourteen of its black officers received medals for heroism.

By the 1930s, most African-American soldiers performed only caretaking jobs. The 10th Cavalry was stationed at Fort Leavenworth. Fort Leavenworth, like other Army posts at that time, was strictly segregated. Black and white soldiers lived in separate quarters.

Buffalo Soldiers guard Mexican prisoners during the search for Pancho Villa.

69

The men of this proud regiment, which had fought with honor, bravery, and skill, now worked as carpenters, clerks, cooks, and mechanics. They took care of the horses that white officers used.

The Buffalo Soldiers took pride in their work, but they felt discouraged that the Army overlooked their abilities. "We took so many of the hard knocks. We withstood the embarrassments," said Sergeant Elmer E. Robinson, who served with the 10th Cavalry during this period.

As in the past, the cavalrymen saw themselves as ordinary soldiers doing their duty and serving their country. Their long, outstanding record helped other African Americans to gain opportunities in the military. "The contribution that we made as black soldiers," explained Robinson, "made it possible for some of the people to be in the position that they are today."

In 1940, the Buffalo Soldiers learned that Benjamin O. Davis, Sr., had become the nation's first black general. Months later, in December 1941, the United States entered World War II. American forces fought against Japan in the South Pacific. They also battled Germany and Italy in Europe and North Africa. And black soldiers made important gains.

Colonel Benjamin O. Davis, Jr., the general's son, commanded the 99th Pursuit Squadron,

America's first squadron of black fighter pilots.

Fighting on horseback had become a thing of the past. The Army no longer needed its cavalry regiments. The soldiers of the 9th and 10th Cavalry transferred to other units. Some were part of the one million African Americans who helped the United States and its allies win World War II.

The war ended in 1945. Three years later, President Harry S Truman ordered an end to segregation in the nation's armed forces. Black and white military personnel served in the same units during the Korean War, from 1950 to 1953. They were among the soldiers of sixteen nations who helped the nation of South Korea fight off an invasion from communist North Korea.

In the Vietnam War of the 1960s and 1970s, U.S. forces again tried to help a small nation— South Vietnam—repel a communist invasion. In this case, the invader was North Vietnam. America's black men and women in Vietnam earned a record worthy of pride. One of every five Congressional Medals of Honor awarded in that war went to an African American.

Opportunities continue to improve. In 1989, President George Bush appointed General Colin Powell as chairman of the Joint Chiefs of Staff. A black soldier now held the nation's highest military post.

People have also looked back into history, to honor black soldiers from the past. Some caring Americans have worked on behalf of the Buffalo Soldiers, gaining them long-overdue honors.

One of those Americans was Ray MacColl, a teacher from Georgia. In 1970, MacColl took a course in black history. He learned of the Buffalo Soldiers and of Henry Flipper, the African-American officer who had been dishonorably discharged at Fort Davis.

MacColl read as much as he could about Flipper's case and tried to clear the deceased soldier's record. Working with Flipper's niece, Irsle King, MacColl organized the details of Flipper's case and presented an appeal to the Army. This time the Army listened. In 1976, Henry Flipper received his honorable discharge.

Another American who worked on behalf of the Buffalo Soldiers was General Colin Powell. In 1982, Powell was stationed at Fort Leavenworth. Out for a jog one morning, Powell noticed two alleyways named 9th and 10th Cavalry streets. These, and a stained glass window in the chapel, were the only memorials to the Buffalo Soldiers at Fort Leavenworth. "I believed we should have something more to commemorate these heroes of the American west," Powell said.

Powell began the project to create the Buffalo

Soldier Monument. Commander Carlton Philpot of the Navy took over the project when Powell left Fort Leavenworth for a new assignment. The more Philpot learned of their history, the more he admired the men of the early black regiments. "Imagine the patriotism it takes to serve your country when your country is treating you unfairly," he said. "These were true patriots."

On July 25, 1992, Colin Powell again faced a crowd at Fort Leavenworth. Behind him stood a bronze statue of a black cavalryman, pulling the reins of his horse. The Buffalo Soldier Monument was now completed. Powell had come to Fort Leavenworth to speak at the dedication ceremony.

Powell asked the crowd to imagine this lone rider "in his coat of blue, on his horse, a soldier of the nation." Possessing strength and courage, "he was every bit the soldier that his white brother was," Powell said.

"Thousands of other brave black Americans have gone into harm's way for their country since the days of the Buffalo Soldier, always moving forward and upward, step by step, sacrifice by sacrifice," Powell continued. "This monument is more than a symbol of African Americans in the military and more than a symbol of American history. The soldier you see here represents all of our beloved America—what we were in the past, what we are

"Imagine the patriotism it takes to serve your country when your country is treating you unfairly. These were true patriots."

now, and, most important of all, what we must be tomorrow."

The monument has a purpose, Powell said. That purpose is "to motivate us to keep struggling until all Americans have a seat at our national table, until all Americans enjoy every opportunity to excel, every chance to achieve their dream."

The Buffalo Soldier
Monument, Fort
Leavenworth, Kansas

Chronology

African Americans in the U.S. Armed Forces

1770	On March 5, Crispus Attucks, a former slave, is among the first to die in the "Boston Massacre."
1776-1781	7,000 African-American soldiers and sailors take part in the Revolutionary War.
1776	On January 16, the Continental Congress agrees to enlist free blacks.
1812-1815	Black soldiers and sailors fight against the British troops at such critical battles as Lake Erie and New Orleans.
1862-1865	186,000 African-American soldiers serve in black regiments during the Civil War; 38,000 black soldiers lose their lives in more than 400 battles.
1862	On July 17, the U.S. Congress approves the enlistment of black soldiers.
1865	On March 13, the Confederate States of America begins to accept black recruits.
1866-1890	Units of black soldiers, referred to as Buffalo Soldiers, are formed as part of the U.S. Army.
1872	On September 21, John H. Conyers becomes the first African American admitted to the U.S. Naval Academy.
1877	On June 15, Henry O. Flipper becomes the first African American to graduate from West Point.
1914-1918	More than 400,000 African Americans serve in the U.S. armed forces during the First World War.

On May 15, two black soldiers, Henry Johnson and Needham Roberts become the first Americans to receive the French Medal of Honor *(Croix de Guerre)*.	1918
In June, Benjamin O. Davis, Jr., graduates from West Point, the first black American to do so in the twentieth century.	1936
Benjamin O. Davis, Sr., becomes the first African-American general in the active Regular Army.	1940
American forces in World War II include more than a million African-American men and women.	1941-1945
On March 25, the Army Air Corps forms its first black unit, the 99th Pursuit Squadron.	1941
On August 24, Colonel Benjamin O. Davis, Jr., is made commander of the 99th Pursuit Squadron.	1942
On January 27 and 28, the airmen of the 99th Pursuit Squadron score a major victory against enemy fighters at the Italian seaside town of Anzio.	1944
On February 2, President Harry S Truman signs Executive Order 9981, ordering an end to segregation in the U.S. armed forces.	1948
Black and white forces fight side by side in Korea as separate black fighting units are disbanded.	1950-1953
Twenty African-American soldiers are awarded the Congressional Medal of Honor during the Vietnam War.	1965-1973
On April 28, Samuel L. Gravely becomes the first black admiral in the history of the U.S. Navy.	1971
In August, Daniel "Chappie" James becomes the first African American to achieve the rank of four-star general.	1975
On October 3, Colin Powell becomes the first African-American chairman of the Joint Chiefs of Staff.	1989
100,000 African-American men and women are sent to the Middle East during the Persian Gulf conflict.	1990-1991
On July 25, the Buffalo Soldier Monument is dedicated at Fort Leavenworth, Kansas.	1992

Index

Bibliography

Brown, Dee. *Bury My Heart at Wounded Knee: An Indian History of the American West.* New York: Bantam Books, 1970.

Buffalo Soldiers at Fort Leavenworth in the 1930s and Early 1940s: Interviews Conducted by Major George E. Knapp. Fort Leavenworth, KS: U.S. Army Command and General Staff College, 1991.

Caroll, John M., ed. *Black Military Experience in the American West.* New York: Liveright Publishing, 1971.

Downie, Fairfax. *The Buffalo Soldiers in the Indian Wars.* New York: McGraw-Hill Books, 1969.

The Guy V. Henry Papers. Held by U.S. Army Military History Institute, Carlisle Barracks, PA.

Leckie, William H. *The Buffalo Soldiers: A Narrative of the Negro Cavalry in the West.* Norman, OK: University of Oklahoma Press, 1967.

Maraniss, David. "Due Recognition and Reward." *The Washington Post,* January 20, 1991.

Order of the Indian Wars. Held by U.S. Army Military History Institute, Carlisle Barracks, PA.

Powell, Colin L. Remarks at the ground-breaking ceremony for the Buffalo Soldier Monument. Fort Leavenworth, Kansas, July 28, 1990.

"Report from Fort Sill, Indian Territory." *Army and Navy Journal,* November 8, 1873.

Wakin, Edward. *Black Fighting Men in U.S. History.* New York: Lothrop, Lee & Shepard, 1971.

"The Buffalo Soldiers." Episode of the Arts & Entertainment Network television series "Time Machine with Jack Perkins."